Conte

Introduction	1	Kookaburra	38
Alphabet Song	6	La Cucaracha	39
A Hunting We Will Go	7	Little Jack Horner	40
A Sailor Went to Sea	8	London Bridge	41
Acka Backa	9	Mary Had a Little Lamb	42
Are You Sleeping?	10	Miss Mary Mack	43
Baa Baa Black Sheep	12	My Hat	44
Baby Bumble Bee	13	Ninety-Nine Bottles	45
Bell Horses	14	Ode to Joy	46
Bim Bum Biddy	15	Oh Susannah	47
Bobby Shafto	16	Oh We Can Play on the Big Bass	
Brahms Lullaby	17	Drum	48
Chumbara	18	Old Bald Eagle	49
Cobbler, Mend My Shoe	19	Old Blue	50
Cock-a-Doodle Doo	20	Old McDonald	51
Ding Dong DiggiDiggiDong	21	Old Mother Hubbard	52
Do You Know the Muffin Man?	22	One, Two, Three, Four	53
Doggie Doggie	23	Rain, Rain, Go Away	54
Fiddle-Dee-Dee	24	Ring Around the Rosie	55
Five Little Ducks	25	Row Row Your Boat	56
Five Little Monkeys	26	Rub-a-Dub-Dub	57
Frog in the Meadow	27	See-Saw Margery Daw	58
Happy Birthday	28	Ten in the Bed	59
Hot Cross Buns	29	The Bee and the Pup	60
Humpty Dumpty	30	The Big Sheep	61
I Like to Eat Apples and Bananas	31	The Mulberry Bush	62
I Love Little Kitty	32	The Wheels on the Bus	63
It's Raining	33	This Old Man	64
Itsy Bitsy Spider	34	Tinga Layo	65
Jack and Jill	35	To Market, To Market	66
Jingle Bells	36	Twinkle, Twinkle Little Star	67
Jolly Old Saint Nicholas	37	We Wish You a Merry Christmas	68

The steel tongue drum (aka tong drum, tank drum, gluck-o-phone, hapi drum) and the hand-pan (aka hank drum, UFO drum, zen drum) are percussion musical instruments designed to help you focus on your feelings, sensations and body. You don't need classical music training or knowledge of music theory to play them. The main purpose is relaxation, meditation and traveling through your inner world.

No previous training or skills are necessary to enjoy these fascinating instruments. It is impossible to play them incorrectly. Anyone can play them: those who want to develop a good sense of rhythm and an ear for music, those who are seeking relaxation after a hard day at work, those who have always had an interest in learning how to play a musical instrument, and those who want to introduce something unusual into their lives and explore their inner selves.

Both instruments have a unique deep and long sound, and both will sound equally good whether under the experienced musician's hands or a beginner's. Playing the handpan/tongue drum is an intuitive experience which transcends gender, age, culture, and language. It is used by hobbyists, performers, music therapists, cancer patients, educators, and students. You can play it too!

The Handpan

The handpan was designed in Berne, Switzerland by Felix Rohner and Sabina Schärer of PANArt in 2000. The original handpan is famous for its beautiful and deep sound, and although the original instrument is no longer produced, demand for it continues to grow. For this reason, the original PANArt handpan is a collector's item, and often difficult to find.

The handpan is a steel instrument which is played while resting on the musician's lap. It is constructed from two joined and shaped solid steel sheets, sealed around the edges to create a hollow cavity inside, and hammered to create perfect tonal fields. It can produce seven to nine specific tones, but unlike the steel drums that are synonymous with Carribean music, the handpan goes through a special process called gas-nitriding which hardens the bowls to create an even more exquisite ethereal sound.

The creation of the handpan was based on the design of other instruments such as gongs, gamelan, ghatam, drums, and bells. The width of the instrument metal is approximately 1mm The drum vibrates and produces sound depending on the size and shape that is hammered into the steel. Accordingly, the tuning is a very technical and time consuming process. Normally, there are 9 notes: an eight note scale around the sides and a lower note in the middle. At the bottom of the instrument (known as the "Gu" side), a hole allows the sound to resonate and to be properly amplified thanks to the phenomenon known as Helmholtz Resonance in physics. This resonance that gives the handpan its distinctive sound is the same property that one experiences when blowing across the top of a glass bottle.

The Steel Tongue Drum

The steel tongue drum evolved from the handpan and the wooden tongue drum, which was invented by the Aztecs in Mexico. Other names used for this instrument are the log drum or tone drum. Traditionally the instrument was made from a hollowed log with tuned tongues. The modern version has tongues cut into the top and can be played with mallets, as well as one's hands. The steel tongue drum is a new invention and it is also called the tank drum because some drums were made from a gas tank.

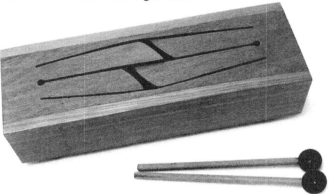

The steel tongue drum gets its unique tone from the vibrations of its tongues of steel. Like the wooden version of this instrument, when the tongue is struck with the finger or a mallet, it vibrates, creating sound waves. The tongues are optimally shaped to achieve the perfect tone and are arranged in such a way that the surrounding notes are musically compatible with each other. By doing this, harmony is created between the notes generated from a particular tongue and the supporting notes of those surrounding it. The multiple harmonic overtones are similar to that of singing bowls or musical bells, and the drum's body creates a resonating chamber that adds depth to the sound.

Main Differences between the Steel Tongue Drum and the Handpan

Both the handpan and the steel tongue drum can be played with your hands and used in your lap. While each instrument has its own unique and special sound, there are some differences:

* The steel tongue drum's notes are sustained for longer periods, usually around 8 seconds. The handpan rings for approximately 4 seconds.
  The handpan has hammered and distorted strike zones. The tongue drum has cut ones.

- A handpan is single-scale tuned and can never be re-tuned. However, while this is true of tongue drums, some new models have multi-scaled tongues that can be re-tuned by adjusting the magnet on the drum.

- The handpan is large (about 24 inches in diameter). The tongue drum is significantly smaller.

- Handpans are more expensive than tongue drums.

- A handpan is very fragile due to its light composite material and the hammered strikes zones. Tongue drums are made of steel.

- The handpan is of African origin, while the tongue drum originated in the Aztec civilization of Mexico.

- The handpan is played by hand, while the steel tongue-drum is sometimes played with mallets, producing a softer sound, almost like raindrops. However, experienced steel tongue drum players can play it using their hands or fingers.

Playing the Steel Tongue Drum

It is important to become acquainted with your steel tongue drum. The sound of the steel tongue drum comes from the vibration of the tongues or slits that are cut out of the top of the instrument.

Tongue drums differ from the handpan in the number of notes and the types of notes which are included on the instrument. Usually, it is a diatonic instrument with one octave plus several notes from other octaves or some chromatic notes. Some may have three C notes and not a single F note. Others have several chromatic notes included.

So while it is based on the regular major diatonic scale, it does not have the typical CDEFGAB arrangement: it can have missing notes, a few additional bass and treble notes placed further away from the main group, or the notes arranged in a variety of ways.

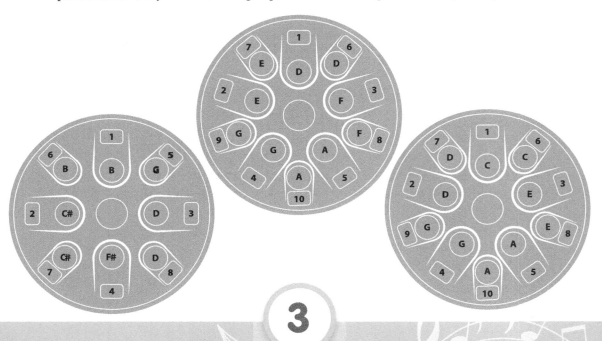

Most steel tongue drums come with mallets. In fact, if you've never played a percussion instrument before, this is the recommended way of playing. With mallets, it is very easy to produce beautiful notes without any effort. Mallets bounce easily on the notes, producing a very clear and deep sound.

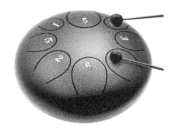

Playing with your hands is more enjoyable, but as mentioned, it requires more technical skill and practice. Most popular models of tongue drum have 6 to 15 notes and come in different sizes, from 5.5 to 20 inches. They can be in many tones: major, minor, pentatonic. Some drums have hole octave notes, while some do not. Very often small drums do not include the note F but the notes C, D and E exist in two different octaves. If your model doesn't have the F note (4), just skip the songs that need this note. Fortunately, most songs assembled here don't use it.

It is important to consider the size of your steel tongue drum. Generally, a smaller drum produces a different sound than that of the larger ones. Most people prefer the sounds produced by larger tongue drums. If you're looking for a more powerful and intense sound, the bigger the instrument, the more volume and reverb it will produce.

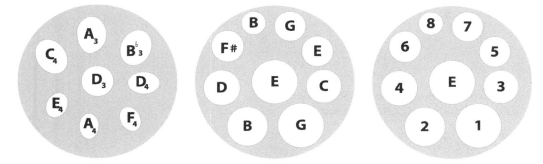

Our book is for those who want to try playing simple popular tunes, and not just relax. As mentioned, the keys are tuned in different notes and you need to understand what notes your particular instrument has. Depending on your instrument, you can skip those songs that contain notes that are missing on your specific drum.

To understand what notes your drum has, you need to look at the instructions. Sometimes the notes are indicated by numbers directly on the keys. Stickers with numbers are sometimes included with the drum.

Hand Playing Technique

- Begin to play with mallets, and then play with your hands. Don't wear rings or any other jewelry while playing.
- Your finger should maintain contact with the surface of the drum for a very short time. The shorter the time of contact with the surface, the longer the sound becomes.
- The quicker your fingers bounce up the drum keys, the richer the overtones will be. Avoid putting your fingers in the middle of the tongue.
- Use the palm to produce force or to extinguish the sound.
- Experiment with different sounds and melodies. No rules - just play whatever you like.

Play by Number

For tongue drums that have numbered musical notation, numbers 1 to 7 represent the keys of the diatonic major scale. For example, a C Major scale would be:

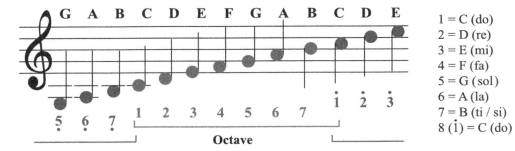

1 = C (do)
2 = D (re)
3 = E (mi)
4 = F (fa)
5 = G (sol)
6 = A (la)
7 = B (ti / si)
8 (1̇) = C (do)

Dots above or below the numbers indicate a note from a higher or lower octave, respectively.

Your drum can be numbered from 1 to 8, where 8 is note C of the next octave. We use number 1 with a dot above the digit for this note because the most popular models of tongue drums use this numeration.

This book is aimed at those who want to add popular melodies to their experimentation. All songs in this book have been written without using the classic music score system, because it is for the absolute beginner who cannot read sheet music.

We use circles with numbers because most modern tongue drums have numbers engraved or painted on their keys. We do not show the note duration - we just group the circles closer to each other to show the rhythms. You can experiment with duration on your own.

Because most tongue drums include and are tuned to involve the notes of the main octave, all songs from this book are possible to play in one octave. If you have less than 1 octave of keys on your drum, you may need to skip some songs. Each tongue drum is very different and it is impossible to accommodate songs for all kinds of tongue drums in one book.

This book includes very simple, popular children's and folk songs, but even well-known children's songs played on the drum will create an unusual magical sound.

Alphabet Song

① ① ⑤ ⑤   ⑥ ⑥ ⑤   ④ ④ ③ ③

A - B - C - D   E - F - G   H - I - J - K

② ② ② ② ①   ⑤ ⑤ ④   ③ ③ ②

L - M - N - O - P   Q - R - S   T - U - V

⑤ ⑤ ④   ③ ③ ②   ① ① ⑤ ⑤

W - X   Y and Z.   Now I know my

⑥ ⑥ ⑤   ④ ④ ③ ③ ② ② ①

A   B   C's.   Next time won't you sing with me.

A Hunting We Will Go

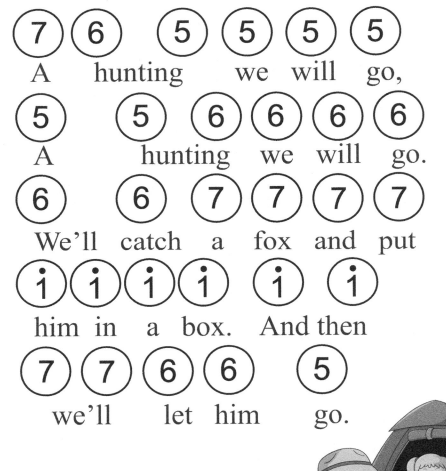

⑦ ⑥ ⑤ ⑤ ⑤ ⑤
A   hunting   we   will   go,

⑤ ⑤ ⑥ ⑥ ⑥ ⑥
A   hunting   we   will   go.

⑥ ⑥ ⑦ ⑦ ⑦ ⑦
We'll   catch   a   fox   and   put

①̇ ①̇ ①̇ ①̇ ①̇ ①̇
him   in   a   box.   And then

⑦ ⑦ ⑥ ⑥ ⑤
we'll   let   him   go.

*The dots above the numbers
mean the notes of another
octave (not the main octave).

7

A Sailor Went to Sea

(5) (1̇) (5)   (6) (5)   (3) (5)   (5) (5)

A   sailor   went to   sea, sea,   sea, to

(6) (5)   (6) (7)   (1̇) (1̇)   (1̇) (5)

see what   he could   see, see,   see, but

(1̇) (5)   (6) (5)   (3) (5)   (5) (5)   (5)

all that   he could   see, see,   see, was   the

(6) (6) (6) (6)   (7) (7)   (1̇) (1̇)   (1̇)

bottom of the deep blue   sea, sea,   sea.

8

Acka Backa

(5) (5) (6) (6)   (5) (5) (3) (3)
Acka   Backa   soda   cracker

(5) (5) (6) (6)   (5)
Acka   Backa   Boo.

(5) (5) (6) (6)   (5) (5) (3) (3)
Acka   Backa   soda   cracker

(5)   (5)   (3)
Out   goes   you!

Are You Sleeping?

(1) (2) (3) (1)   (1) (2) (3) (1)
Are you sleeping,   are you sleeping?

(3) (4) (5)   (3) (4) (5)
Brother John, Brother John?

(5) (6) (5) (4) (3) (1)
Morning bells are ringing,

(5) (6) (5) (4) (3) (1)
Morning bells are ringing

(2) (5) (1)   (2) (5) (1)
Ding ding dong,   ding ding dong.

⑤ ⑥ ⑦ ⑤ ⑤ ⑥ ⑦ ⑤
Are you sleeping, are you sleeping?

⑦ ①̇ ②̇ ⑦ ①̇ ②̇
Brother John, Brother John?

②̇ ③̇ ②̇ ①̇ ⑦ ⑤
Morning bells are ringing,

②̇ ③̇ ②̇ ①̇ ⑦ ⑤
Morning bells are ringing

⑥ ② ⑤ ⑥ ② ⑤
Ding ding dong, ding ding dong.

Baa Baa Black Sheep

(1) (1) (5) (5) (6) (6) (6) (6) (5)

Baa, Baa, black sheep, have you any wool?

(4) (4) (3) (3) (2) (2) (1)

Yes sir, yes sir, three bags full.

(5) (5) (5) (4) (4) (3) (3) (3) (2)

One for the master, one for the dame,

(5) (5) (5) (4) (4) (4) (4)

one for the little boy, who

(3) (3) (3) (2)

lives down the lane.

12

Baby Bumble Bee

① ④ ⑥ ⑤ ④ ② ② ① ① ④

I'm bringing home a   baby   bumble bee

⑤   ⑤ ⑥ ⑥ ⑤ ⑥ ⑤ ③ ②

Won't my mommy be   so proud of me,

① ④ ⑥ ⑤ ④ ② ②

I'm bringing home a   baby

① ① ④

bumble bee.

Bell Horses

⑤ ③ ③ ⑤ ③ ③

Bell   horses,   bell   horses,

⑤ ⑤ ⑥ ⑥ ⑤

What's the   time of   day?

⑤ ⑤ ③ ⑤ ⑤ ③

One o'clock,   two o'clock,

⑤ ⑤ ⑥ ⑥ ⑤

Time   to   go   away.

Bim Bum Biddy

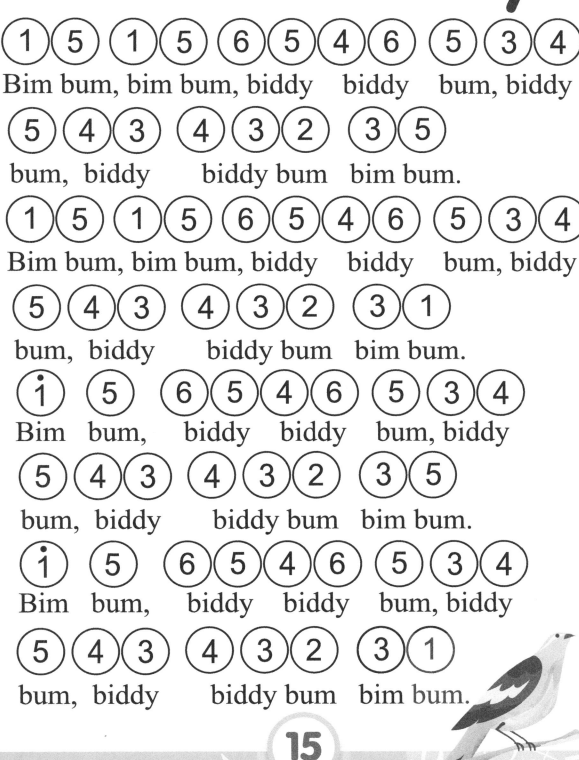

(1)(5) (1)(5) (6)(5)(4)(6) (5)(3)(4)
Bim bum, bim bum, biddy   biddy   bum, biddy

(5)(4)(3) (4)(3)(2) (3)(5)
bum, biddy   biddy bum   bim bum.

(1)(5) (1)(5) (6)(5)(4)(6) (5)(3)(4)
Bim bum, bim bum, biddy   biddy   bum, biddy

(5)(4)(3) (4)(3)(2) (3)(1)
bum, biddy   biddy bum   bim bum.

(1̇) (5) (6)(5)(4)(6) (5)(3)(4)
Bim   bum,   biddy   biddy   bum, biddy

(5)(4)(3) (4)(3)(2) (3)(5)
bum, biddy   biddy bum   bim bum.

(1̇) (5) (6)(5)(4)(6) (5)(3)(4)
Bim   bum,   biddy   biddy   bum, biddy

(5)(4)(3) (4)(3)(2) (3)(1)
bum, biddy   biddy bum   bim bum.

15

Bobby Shafto

(5)(5) (6)(6) (5)(5) (3)

Bobby Shafto's gone to sea,

(5)(5) (6)(6) (5)(5) (3)

Silver   buckles   on   his   knee.

(5)(5) (6)(6) (5)(5) (3)

He'll come back and marry me.

(5)(5) (6)(6) (5)(3)

Bonnie   Bobby   Shafto!

Brahms' Lullaby

③ ③⑤ ③ ③ ⑤

Lullaby,   and   good night,

③ ⑤ ①⑦⑥⑥⑤

With   pink   roses   bedight,

② ③④②②③④

With   lilies   o'er   spread,

②④⑦⑥ ⑤⑦①

Is my   baby's   sweet head.

① ① ① ⑥ ④ ⑤

Lay   you   down   now,   and   rest,

③ ① ④ ⑤ ⑥ ⑤

May   your   slumber   be   blessed!

① ① ① ⑥ ④ ⑤

Lay   you   down   now,   and   rest,

③ ① ④ ③ ② ①

May   your   slumber   be   blessed!

Chumbara

(1)(1)(1)(3)(2)(1)

Chumbara,　chumbara,

(5)(5)(5)(5)(4)(3)

chumbara,　chumbara

(2)(2)(2)(4)(3)(2)

Chumbara,　chumbara,

(1)(i)(7)(6)(5)(4)(3)(2)

chum, chum, chum, chum, chum, chum

(1)(1)(1)(3)(2)(1)

Chumbara,　chumbara,

(5)(5)(5)(5)(4)(3)

chumbara,　chumbara

(2)(2)(2)(4)(3)(2)(1)(i)(1)

Chumbara, chumbara, chum, chum, chum

Cobbler, Mend My Shoe

(1)(1)(5)(5)(6)(6)(5)(4)(4)(3)(3)

Cobbler, cobbler, mend my shoe. Get it done by

(2)(2)(1) (5)(5)(4)(4)(3)(3)(2)

half past two. Stitch it up and stitch it down

(5)(5)(4)(4)(3)(3)(2) (1)(1)(5)(5)

then I'll give you half a crown. Cobbler, cobbler,

(6)(6)(5) (4)(4)(3)(3) (2)(2)(1)

mend my shoe. Get it done by half past two.

19

Cock-a-Doodle Doo

①③③②③③①③③②③
Cock-a-doodle doo, my dame has lost her shoe,

③①̇①̇⑦⑥⑤③①②
and master's lost his fiddling stick and

③ ⑤③②①① ①③ ③②
doesn't know what to do. And doesn't know what to

③③ ⑤⑥ ⑤③⑤⑤
do. and doesn't know what to do. The

①̇①̇⑦⑥⑤③①②
master's lost his fiddling stick and

③ ⑤③②①
doesn't know what to do.

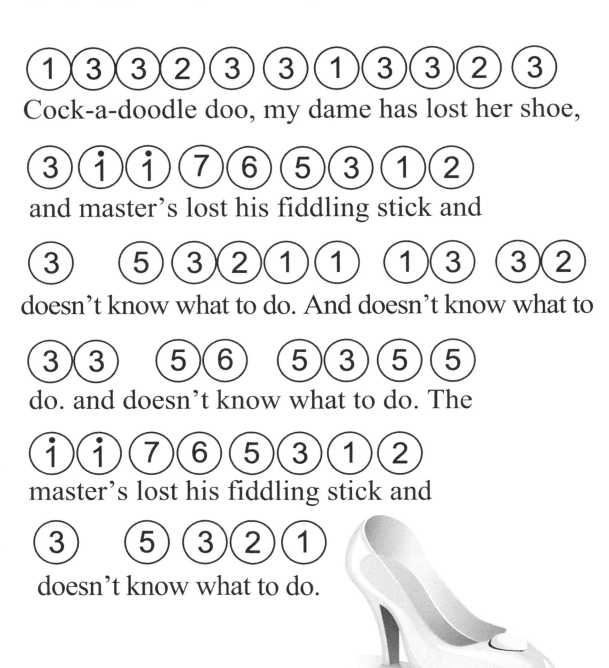

Ding Dong DiggiDiggiDong

(i) (5) (6)(6)(6)(6) (5)

Ding, dong, diggidiggi dong

(3)(3)(3)(3) (2)(3) (1)(1) (5)

Diggidiggi dong, the cat, she's gone!

(i) (5) (6)(6)(6)(6) (5)

Ding, dong, diggidiggi dong,

(3)(3)(3)(3) (2) (3) (1)

Diggi diggi ding, dang dong.

Do You Know the Muffin Man?

(1) (1) (4) (4) (5) (6) (4) (4)
Oh, do you know the muf-fin man,

(3) (2) (5) (5) (4) (3) (1) (1)
The muf-fin man, the muf-fin man.

(1) (1) (4) (4) (5) (6) (4) (4)
Oh, do you know the muf-fin man,

(4) (5) (5) (1) (1) (4)
That lives on Dru-ry Lane?

Doggie Doggie

(5) (5) (3) (3) (5) (5) (3)

Doggie,   doggie, where's your bone?

(5) (5)(5) (3) (6) (5) (5) (3)

Somebody   stole   it   from your home.

(5) (3)(6) (5) (3)

Who has my   bone?

(5) (3)(6) (5) (3)

I   have your   bone.

Fiddle-Dee-Dee

(3)(1)(1)(1)(3)(1)(1)(1)(1)

Fiddle dee dee, Fiddle dee dee, The

(2)(2)(5)(5)(5)(3)(1)(1)(1)(1)

fly has married the bumble bee. Said the

(6)(6)(6)(6)(6)(6)(5)(5)(5)

fly, said he, "Will you marry me? And

(5)(4)(4)(5)(4)(3)(3)(3)(1)(1)(1)

live with me, sweet bumble bee?" Fiddle dee dee,

(3)(1)(1)(1)(1)(2)(2)(5)(5)(5)

Fiddle dee dee, The fly has married the

(3)(1)(1)

bumble bee.

Five Little Ducks

(3) (2) (2) (1) (i) (7) (6) (5)

Five   little ducks went out one day,

(5) (1) (1) (4) (3) (3) (2) (2)

Over   the hill and   far   away

(3) (3) (2) (1)   (i)   (7)   (6)   (5)   (5)

Mother duck said, "Quack, quack, quack, quack", and

(5) (1)   (4) (3) (3)   (2)   (2) (1)

only   four   little   ducks came back.

Five Little Monkeys

① ⑥ ⑥ ⑤ ⑥ ① ① ⑥ ⑥ ⑤

Five little monkeys jumping on the bed,

① ⑥ ⑤ ⑥ ③ ② ① ①

one fell off and bumped his head. So

① ① ⑥ ⑥ ⑤ ⑤ ⑥ ⑥ ① ⑥ ⑤

momma called the doctor and the doctor said,

①̇ ⑥ ⑤ ⑥ ③ ③ ② ② ①

"No more monkey jumping one the bed!"

26

Frog in the Meadow

(7) (7) (7) (6) (5)

Frog in the meadow,

(7) (7) (7) (5)

can't get him out.

(7) (7) (7) (7) (6) (5)

Take a little stick and

(7) (7) (7) (5)

stir him about.

Happy Birthday

(1) (1) (2)   (1) (4) (3)

Happy   birthday   to   you,

(1) (1) (2)   (1) (5) (4)

Happy   birthday   to   you,

(1) (1) (i̇)   (6) (4) (4) (3) (2)

Happy   birthday   dear   Mary,

(i̇) (i̇) (6)   (4) (5) (4)

Happy   birthday   to   you!

Hot Cross Buns

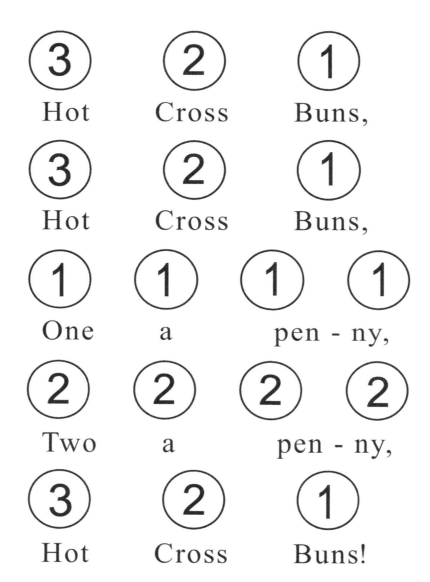

③   ②   ①
Hot   Cross   Buns,

③   ②   ①
Hot   Cross   Buns,

①   ①   ①   ①
One   a   pen - ny,

②   ②   ②   ②
Two   a   pen - ny,

③   ②   ①
Hot   Cross   Buns!

Humpty Dumpty

③⑤ ④⑥ ⑤⑥⑦ ①
Humpty Dumpty sat on   a   wall,

③⑤ ④⑥ ⑤③① ②
Humpty Dumpty had a great   fall;

③③⑤ ④④⑥ ⑤⑥⑦ ①
All the king's horses and all the king's men

③̇③̇①̇ ④̇④̇③̇ ②̇①̇⑦ ①̇
Couldn't   put Humpty together again.

I Like to Eat Apples and Bananas

(3̇)(5̇)(3̇) (1̇)(1̇)(1̇) (3̇)(2̇)(3̇)(4̇)

I   like to   eat, eat, eat   apples and ba-

(3̇)(2̇)   (2̇)(4̇)(2̇)(7)(7)(7)

nanas,   I   like   to   eat, eat,   eat

(2̇)(1̇)(2̇)(3̇) (2̇)(1̇)   (3̇)(5̇)(3̇)

apples and ba   - nanas   I   like to

I Love Little Kitty

③ ④ ⑤ ⑤ ⑤ ⑤ ⑴ ⑦ ⑥ ② ②

I   love little   kitty, Her coat is so

② ③ ④ ④ ④ ④ ④ ⑦ ⑥

warm, And if I don't hurt her, She'll

⑤ ③ ③ ③ ③ ④ ⑤ ⑤ ⑤

do me no   harm. So I'll not pull her

⑤ ⑴ ⑦ ⑥ ② ② ② ② ③

tail, Nor   drive her a-way, But

④ ⑦ ⑥ ⑤ ③̇ ②̇ ⑴ ① ① ①

kitty and   I, very   gently will play.

It's Raining

(5) (5) (3) (6) (5) (3) (3)

It's raining, it's pouring, the

(5) (3) (6) (5) (3)

old man is snoring.

(5) (5) (3) (3) (6) (5) (5) (3) (3) (6)

Went to bed and he bumped his head and he

(5) (5) (5) (3) (3) (6) (5) (3)

couldn't get up in the morning.

33

Itsy Bitsy Spider

(1) (1) (1) (1) (2) (3) (3)

The   itsy - bitsy   spider

(3)   (2)   (1)   (2)(3)   (1)

Climbed   up   the   water   spout.

(3)   (3)   (4)   (5)

Down   came   the   rain

(5)   (4)   (3)   (4) (5)   (3)

And   washed   the   spider   out.

(1)   (1)   (2)   (3)

Out   came   the   sun

(3)   (2)   (1) (2) (3)   (1)

And   dried   up   all   the   rain

(1)   (1)   (1)   (1)(2)   (3) (3)

And   the itsy - bitsy   spider

(3)   (2)(1)   (2)   (3)(1)

Climbed   up   the   spout   again.

Jack and Jill

(1) (1) (2) (2)   (3) (3) (4) (4)

Jack and Jill went   up   the hill, to

(5) (5) (6) (6)   (7) (i)

fetch a   pail of   water

(i) (i) (7) (7)   (6) (6) (5) (5)

Jack fell down and broke his crown and

(4) (4) (3) (3)   (2) (1)

Jill came tumbling   after.

Jingle Bells

③ ③ ③ ③ ③ ③
Jingle   bells,   jingle bells,

③ ⑤ ① ② ③
Jingle   all the way.

④ ④ ④ ④ ④ ③ ③
Oh, what fun it   is   to ride

③ ③ ② ② ③ ② ⑤
In   a   one horse open   sleigh.

③ ③ ③ ③ ③ ③
Jingle   bells,   jingle bells,

③ ⑤ ① ② ③
Jingle   all the way.

④ ④ ④ ④ ④ ③ ③
Oh, what fun it   is   to ride

③ ⑤ ⑤ ④ ② ①
In a one horse   open   sleigh.

Jolly Old Saint Nicholas

(6) (6) (6) (6)   (5) (5) (5)
Jolly   old Saint   Nicholas

(4) (4) (4) (4) (6)
Lean   your   ear   this   way.

(2) (2) (2) (2) (1) (1) (4)
Don't   you   tell   a   single   soul

(5) (4) (5) (6) (5)
What   I'm going   to say.

(6) (6) (6) (6) (5) (5) (5)
Christmas   Eve   is   coming   soon.

(4) (4) (4) (4) (6)
Now,   you   dear old   man,

(2) (2) (2) (2) (1) (1) (4)
Whisper   what you'll   bring   to   me.

(5) (4) (5) (6) (4)
Tell   me   if   you   can.

MERRY CHRISTMAS

37

Kookaburra

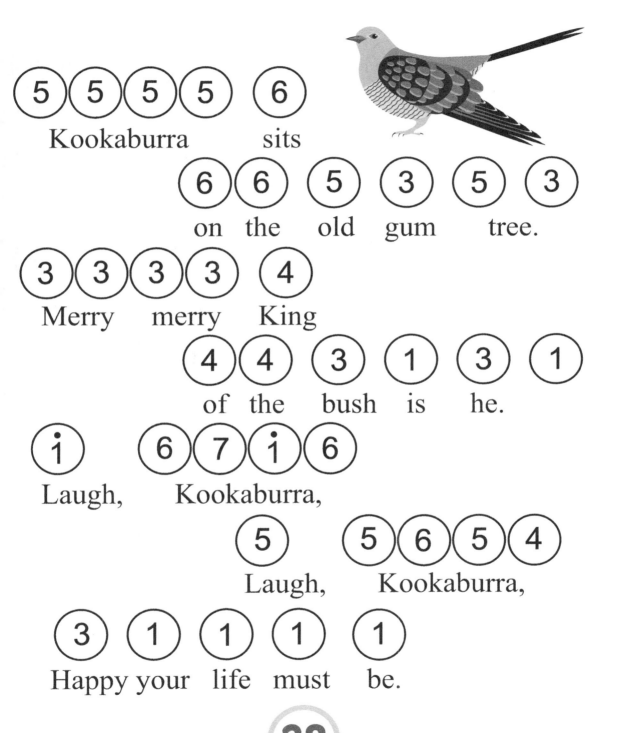

⑤ ⑤ ⑤ ⑤ ⑥
Kookaburra   sits

⑥ ⑥ ⑤ ③ ⑤ ③
on   the   old   gum   tree.

③ ③ ③ ③ ④
Merry   merry   King

④ ④ ③ ① ③ ①
of   the   bush   is   he.

①̇ ⑥ ⑦ ①̇ ⑥
Laugh,   Kookaburra,

⑤ ⑤ ⑥ ⑤ ④
Laugh,   Kookaburra,

③ ① ① ① ①
Happy your   life   must   be.

La Cucaracha

(1) (1) (1) (4) (6) (1) (1) (1) (4) (6)

La   cu - ca - ra - cha,   la   cu - ca - ra - cha

(4)   (4) (3) (3) (2) (2) (1)

Ya   no   puede   caminar,

(1) (1) (1) (3) (5) (1) (1) (1) (3) (5)

Porque   no   tiene,   porque   le   falta

(i)   (i) (i) (i) (6) (5) (4)

Dos   patitos   para   andar.

Little Jack Horner

①①① ④③ ②②② ⑤④
Little Jack Horner sat in the corner,

③③③ ⑥⑤④   ①
Eating   a Christmas pie;   He

①①① ④ ③ ②②② ⑤ ④
put in his thumb, and pulled out a plum, And

③③③ ③②③ ④
said, "What a good boy am   I!"

40

London Bridge
Is Falling Down

(5) (6) (5) (4) (3) (4) (5)

London   Bridge   is   falling   down,

(2) (3) (4) (3) (4) (5)

Falling   down,   falling   down.

(5) (6) (5) (4) (3) (4) (5)

London   Bridge   is   falling   down,

(2) (5) (3) (1)

My   fair   lady.

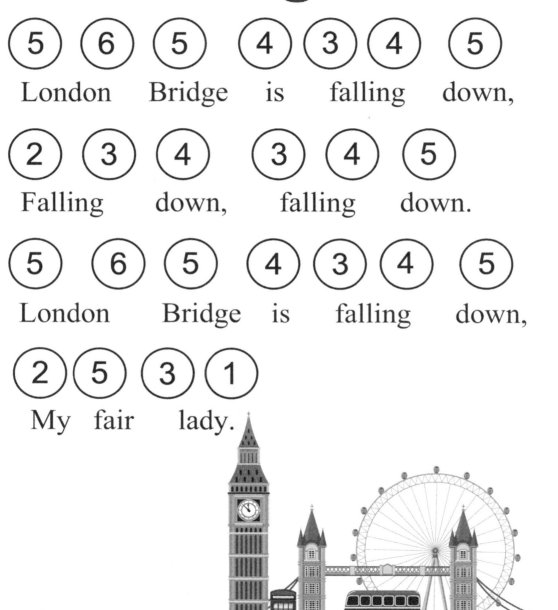

41

Mary Had a Little Lamb

③ ② ① ② ③ ③ ③

Mary had a little lamb,

② ② ② ③ ⑤ ⑤

Little lamb, little lamb,

③ ② ① ② ③ ③ ③

Mary had a little lamb,

③ ② ② ③ ② ①

Its fleece was white as snow.

Miss Mary Mack

(5) (6) (7) (i) (i) (i)

Miss   Mary   Mack, Mack, Mack,

(5) (6) (7) (i) (i) (i)

all   dressed in   black, black, black,

(5)(6)(7)(i)(i)(i)(i)(i)(i)

with   silver   buttons, buttons, buttons

(5) (6) (7) (i) (i) (i)

all   down her   back, back, back!

43

My Hat

(5) (6) (5) (4) (3)   (4) (2)   (3)

My hat   it   has three corners; Three

(4)(5) (6) (5) (3)   (5) (i) (5) (4)(3)

corners has my hat,   And had   it not three

(4)(2)   (3) (4)(5) (6)(5) (1)

corners,   it would not be my   hat.

Ninety-Nine Bottles

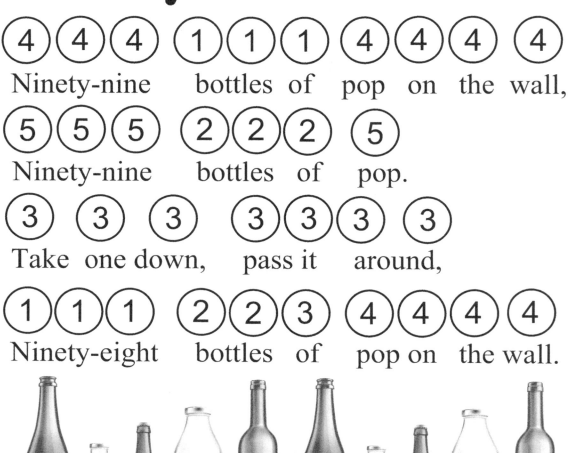

(4)(4)(4) (1)(1)(1) (4)(4)(4) (4)
Ninety-nine   bottles of   pop   on   the   wall,

(5)(5)(5) (2)(2)(2) (5)
Ninety-nine   bottles   of   pop.

(3) (3) (3) (3)(3)(3) (3)
Take one down,   pass it   around,

(1)(1)(1) (2)(2)(3) (4)(4)(4)(4)
Ninety-eight   bottles   of   pop on   the wall.

No more bottles of pop on the wall,
no more bottles of pop.
Go to the store and buy some more,
99 bottles of pop on the wall...

Ode to Joy

(3) (3) (4) (5) (5) (4) (3) (2)

(1) (1) (2) (3) (3) (2)(2)

(3) (3) (4) (5) (5) (4) (3) (2)

(1) (1) (2) (3) (2) (1)(1)

(2) (2) (3) (1) (2) (3)(4)(3) (1)

(2) (3)(4)(3) (2) (1) (2) (5)

(3) (3) (4) (5) (5) (4) (3) (2)

(1) (1) (2) (3) (2) (1)(1)

46

Oh! Susannah

(1) (2) (3) (5) (5)(6)(5)(3)
Well! I come from A-la-ba-ma

(1) (2) (3)(3) (2) (1) (2)
With my ban-jo on my knee,

(1)(2)(3)(5)(5)(6)(5)(3)
I'm going to Louis-i-a-na

(1)(2)(3)(3)(2)(2)(1)
My true love for to see.

(4) (4) (6)(6)
Oh!   Su-san-nah,

(5)   (5) (3)(1)(2)
Don't you cry for me

(1)(2)(3)(5)(5)(6)(5)(3)
I   come from A-la-ba-ma

(1) (2)(3)(3) (2) (2)(1)
With my ban-jo on my knee.

Oh We Can Play on the Big Bass Drum

(1)(3)(5)(5)(5)(5)(6)(5)(3)(1)

Oh we can play on the big bass drum,

(1)(i)(i)(i)(7)(6)(6)(5)

And this is the music to it.

(3)(3)(2)(1)(2)(3)(3)(2)

Boom, boom, boom goes the big gass drum,

(5)(i)(1)(2)(3)(2)(1)

And that's the way we do it.

Old Bald Eagle

(4)(4) (4)(4) (4)(4) (1)

Old bald   eagle   sail around,

(4) (3)(4) (5)

daylight   is   gone.

(3)(3) (3)(3) (3)(3) (1)

Old bald   eagle   sail around,

(6) (6)(5) (4)

daylight   is   gone.

Two bald eagles...

Three bald eagles...

Four bald eagles...

Old Blue

(3)(3)(3)(3)(1)(1)(3)(3)(5)

I had a dog and his name was Blue,

(3)(3)(3)(3)(1)(1)(2)(2)(1)

I had a dog and his name was Blue.

(3)(3)(3)(3)(1)(1)(3)(3)(5)(5)(5)

I had a dog and his name was Blue, And I

(3)(3)(3)(3)(3)(1)(1)(2)(2)(1)

betcha five dollars he's a good dog too.

(5)(3)(1)(2)(2)(1)

Here Blue! You good dog you.

Old MacDonald Had a Farm

⑤ ⑤ ⑤ ② ③ ③ ②
Old McDonald   had a farm.

⑦ ⑦ ⑥ ⑥ ⑤
E - I - E - I - O

② ⑤ ⑤ ⑤ ② ③ ③ ②
And on   that farm he had a cow.

⑦ ⑦ ⑥ ⑥ ⑤
E - I - E - I - O

② ② ⑤ ⑤ ⑤
With a moo moo here.

② ② ⑤ ⑤ ⑤
With a moo moo there.

⑤ ⑤ ⑤
Here a moo.

⑤ ⑤ ⑤
There a moo.

⑤ ⑤ ⑤ ⑤ ⑤ ⑤
Everywhere a moo moo.

⑤ ⑤ ⑤ ② ③ ③ ②
Old McDonald   had a farm.

51

⑦ ⑦ ⑥ ⑥ ⑤
E - I - E - I - O

Old Mother Hubbard

④④④ ④③ ④ ⑤⑤⑤

Old Mother Hubbard, She went to the

⑤④⑤⑥⑥⑥①⑦⑥⑤①

cupboard to get her poor dog a bone. But

④ ④ ④ ④ ④ ⑤⑤ ⑤⑤ ⑤

when she got there the cupboard was bare, And

⑥⑤④③④⑤④

so the poor dog had none.

One, Two, Three, Four

③ ③ ② ① ①
One, two, three, four, five

① ② ③ ⑤ ⑤ ④ ④
once I caught a fish alive.

④ ④ ④ ③ ② ②
Six, seven, eight, nine, ten,

① ⑦ ⑥ ⑦ ② ① ①
then I let it go again.

Rain, Rain, Go Away

(5) (3)　(5) (5) (3)
Rain, rain,　go　away,

(5) (5) (3) (6)　(5) (5) (3)
Come again　a - nother　day,

(4) (4) (2) (2)　(4) (4) (2)
Little　children　wants to　play,

(5) (4) (3) (2)　(3) (1) (1)
Rain,　rain　go　away.

Ring Around the Rosie

⑤ ⑤ ③ ⑥ ⑤ ③ ③

Ring around the rosie, A

⑤ ⑤ ③ ⑥ ⑤ ③

pocket full of posies,

⑤ ③ ⑤ ③ ③

Atishoo! Atishoo! We

⑤ ⑤ ①

all fall down!

Row, Row, Row Your Boat

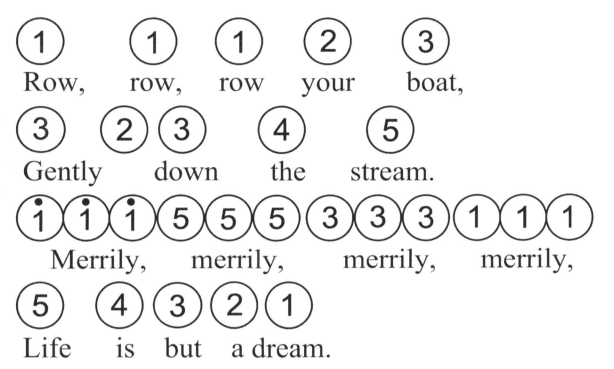

(1) (1) (1) (2) (3)
Row,   row,   row   your   boat,

(3) (2) (3) (4) (5)
Gently   down   the   stream.

(1) (1) (1) (5) (5) (5) (3) (3) (3) (1) (1) (1)
Merrily,   merrily,   merrily,   merrily,

(5) (4) (3) (2) (1)
Life   is   but   a dream.

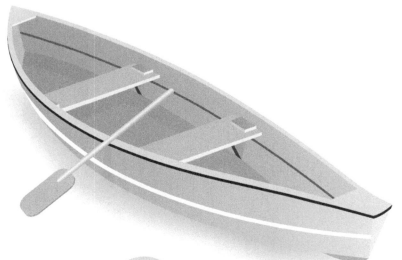

Rub-a-Dub-Dub

(1) (1) (1) (1) (1) (3) (3) (3) (3)

Rub-a-dub - dub, three men in a tub,

(3) (5) (5) (5) (5) (5) (5) (5)

And who do you think they be?

(5) (i) (i) (i) (5) (5) (5)

The butcher, the baker, the

(3) (3) (3) (1) (1) (1)

candlestick maker, and

(5) (5) (4) (3) (2) (1)

all of them gone to sea.

See-Saw Margery Daw

(5) (3) (5) (5) (5) (3)

See-saw, Margery Daw

(5) (5) (3) (3) (6) (5) (3)

Jack shall have a new master.

(5)(5) (3) (3) (3) (5)(5) (5) (3) (3)

He shall have but a penny a day, Be-

(5) (5) (5) (3) (3) (6) (5) (3)

cause he won't work any faster.

Ten in the Bed

① ① ④ ④ ④ ④ ① ①

There were ten in the bed and the

④ ④ ④ ④ î ⑥ ④

little one said, "Roll over,

î ⑥ ④ ① ① ④ ④

"Roll over, So they all rolled

④ ④ ① ④ ④ ④

over and one fell out.

The Bee and the Pup

(5) (5) (3) (1) (1) (1) (1) (1) (5) (5) (3)

There was   a   bee - i - ee - i - ee Sat on   a

(2) (2) (2) (2) (2) (5) (6) (5)

wall-i - all - i - all And he went

(7) (7) (7) (7) (7) (5) (6) (7)

buzz-i - uzz - i -uzz   And that was

(1̇) (1̇) (1̇) (1̇) (1̇)

all - i - all - i - all!

The Big Sheep

(5) (7) (6) (5) (3) (2) (2) (2) (3) (5)

As   I went to   market on   one market

(6) (5) (7) (7) (6) (5) (3) (2) (2)

day, I   saw as   big   a sheep,   sir as

(2) (2) (3) (4) (5) (5) (7) (5) (6) (5)

ever   fed on hay. Oh,   farearaddy

(3) (2) (2) (2) (2) (3) (5) (6) (5)

daddy, Oh   farearaddy   hay. Oh,

(7) (5) (6) (5) (3) (2) (2)

farearaddy   daddy, Oh

(2) (2) (3) (5) (5)

farearaddy   day.

The Mulberry Bush

(4)(4)(4) (4) (6) (i)(i)(6) (4)

Here we go round the   mulberry   bush,

(4) (5)(5)(5) (5) (6) (5)(5)(3) (1)

the   mulberry   bush, the   mulberry   bush,

(4)(4)(4) (4) (6) (i)(i)(6) (4)

Here we go round   the   mulberry   bush,

(4) (5)(5) (1)(2)(3) (4) (4)

so   early   in   the   morning.

The Wheels on the Bus

(1) (4) (4) (4) (4) (6) (i) (6) (4)

The wheels on   the bus   go round and round.

(5) (3) (1)   (i) (6) (4)

Round and round.   Round and round.

(1) (4) (4) (4) (4) (6) (i) (6) (4)

The wheels on   the   bus   go round and round.

(5) (1) (1) (4)

Round and round.

This Old Man

(5)(3)(5) (5)(3)(5) (6)(5) (4)(3)

This old man, he played one, He played knick-knack

(2)(3)(4) (3)(4)(5)(1) (1)(1)(1)

on my thumb; With a knick-knack paddy whack,

(1)(2)(3)(4) (5) (5)(2) (2)(4)

Give the dog a bone! This old man came

(3)(2)(1)

rolling home.

Tinga Layo

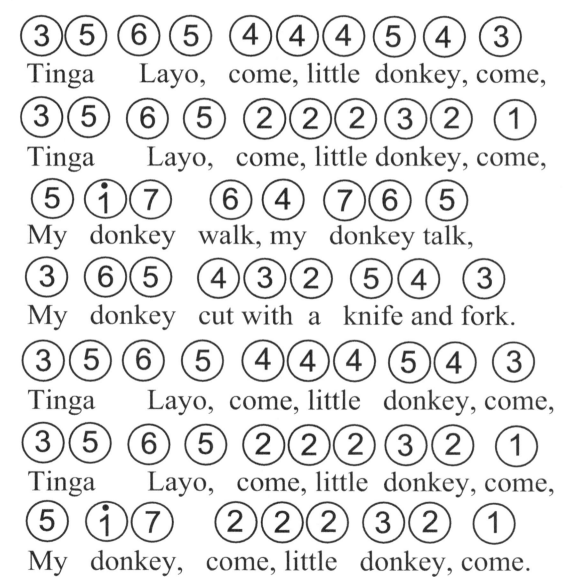

③⑤ ⑥ ⑤ ④④④ ⑤④ ③
Tinga   Layo,   come, little   donkey, come,

③⑤ ⑥ ⑤ ②②② ③② ①
Tinga   Layo,   come, little donkey, come,

⑤ ⓘ⑦   ⑥ ④ ⑦⑥ ⑤
My   donkey   walk, my   donkey talk,

③ ⑥⑤ ④③② ⑤④ ③
My   donkey   cut with a   knife and fork.

③⑤ ⑥ ⑤ ④④④ ⑤④ ③
Tinga   Layo, come, little   donkey, come,

③⑤ ⑥ ⑤ ②②② ③② ①
Tinga   Layo, come, little donkey, come,

⑤ ⓘ⑦ ②②② ③② ①
My   donkey,   come, little   donkey, come.

To Market, To Market

⑤ ① ⑤ ⑤ ① ⑤ ⑤ ③ ② ① ⑤

To market, to market to buy a fat pig.

⑥ ⑦ ① ⑤ ④ ③ ③ ② ① ② ⑤

Home again, home again jiggety jig. To

① ⑤ ⑤ ① ⑤ ⑤ ③ ② ① ⑥

market, to market to buy a fat hog.

⑤ ⑥ ⑦ ① ⑤ ③ ④ ③ ② ①

Home again, home again jiggety jog.

66

Twinkle, Twinkle Little Star

(1) (1) (5) (5) (6) (6) (5)

Twin - kle,   twin - kle   lit - tle   star,

(4) (4) (3) (3)   (2) (2) (1)

How   I   won - der   what   you   are.

(5)(5)(4)   (4)   (3)   (3)(2)

Up   a - bove   the   world   so   high,

(5) (5) (4)   (4)   (3)   (3) (2)

Like   a   dia - mond   in   the   sky.

We Wish You a Merry Christmas

① ④ ④ ⑤ ④ ③ ② ②

We   wish   you   a   Mer - ry   Christ - mas,

② ⑤ ⑤ ⑥ ⑤ ④ ③ ①

We   wish   you   a   Mer - ry   Christ - mas,

① ⑥ ⑥ ⑥ ⑥ ⑤ ④ ②

We   wish   you   a   Mer - ry   Christ - mas,

① ① ② ⑤ ③ ④

And   a   Hap - py   New Year!

68

Made in the USA
Coppell, TX
15 November 2024

40302710R00039